THE MEANING OF BEING HUMAN

THE MEANING OF BEING HUMAN

Synodal Considerations

EDITED BY
Elsie M. Miranda AND
Cristina L. H. Traina

FOREWORD BY
Susan A. Ross

Paulist Press
New York / Mahwah, NJ

Cover image by Flame of life / Shutterstock.com
Cover and book design by Lynn Else

Library of Congress Cataloging-in-Publication Data
Names: Miranda, Elsie M. editor | Traina, Cristina L. H. editor
Title: The meaning of being human: synodal considerations / Cristina L.H. Traina and Elsie M. Miranda; foreword by Susan A. Ross.
Description: New York: Paulist Press, [2025] | Includes bibliographical references. | Summary: "This collection of essays explores the meaning of being human as beloved creatures of God in the context of an ever-evolving creation"— Provided by publisher.
Identifiers: LCCN 2024056202 (print) | LCCN 2024056203 (ebook) | ISBN 9780809157662 paperback | ISBN 9780809189311 ebook
Subjects: LCSH: Catholic Church—Doctrines | Theological anthropology—Catholic Church
Classification: LCC BT701.3 .M39 2025 (print) | LCC BT701.3 (ebook) | DDC 233—dc23/eng/20250603
LC record available at https://lccn.loc.gov/2024056202
LC ebook record available at https://lccn.loc.gov/2024056203

ISBN 978-0-8091-5766-2 (paperback)
ISBN 978-0-8091-8931-1 (ebook)

Published by Paulist Press
997 Macarthur Boulevard
Mahwah, NJ 07430
www.paulistpress.com

Printed and bound in the
United States of America

CONTENTS

FOREWORD

Theological anthropology is the area of theology that explores what it means to be human. For Christians, this means, at minimum, that we are created in the image of God, that our created bodily nature is good, that we fall short of goodness, and that in Christ we have been reconciled with God. In the past, theological anthropology was usually known as the "doctrine of man" and the human being was often described, using Aristotle's terms, as a "rational animal." These ideas tended to look at men—usually Western, white men—as the ideal and normative models for humanity and saw rationality as men's most distinctive feature. Women, by contrast, were seen as "misbegotten males," with a lesser capacity for reasoning, and subject by their nature to male dominance.

In recent years, particularly since Vatican II (1962–65), issues of identity have complicated the discussion of what it means to be human. Instead of beginning with the things that all people hold in common—body, mind, emotions—many contemporary discussions question whether "rational man" is the best way of describing who we are and instead highlight the rich *diversity* of humanity, so as to enrich our understanding of who we are. That is to say, we think of our gender and sexuality not only as either male or female, and "straight," but also within the spectrum of gay, lesbian, bisexual, trans, queer, intersex, or asexual; we consider our culturally constructed and imposed categories of race and ethnicity as central to our often-complex identity; we wonder about our connections to other human and nonhuman living creatures. In short, in order to do justice to the diverse community that is humanity, contemporary theological anthropolo*gies* (note the plural) are now far more complex, multifaceted, and inclusive. One main reason for this shift is the acknowledgment that our experiences shape how we see the world and therefore how we formulate our theologies. There are, to be sure, some who resist this development; the well-documented divisions in the church today are evidence of this.

What are the consequences of such a shift in our theological self-understanding? Consider how the concept of original sin has traditionally been understood. This is the theological acknowledgment not only of our finitude but also of our inability to live perfectly—or, as Augustine (354–430) put it, our inability *not* to sin. As the biblical story of Adam and Eve portrays it, human beings—who "inherit" their tendency to sin from these first parents—disobeyed God's command and "lost" their innocence, resulting in the greatly flawed world in which we live. Theologians such as Augustine and Thomas Aquinas (1225–74) identified pride—basically, putting oneself above others, even above God—as the "original" sin, from which all other sins result, and largely, theologians concurred. But in the last half of the twentieth century, people began to question whether such an understanding adequately reflected their experiences. In other words, are people who have not benefitted from various kinds of power, such as women, colonized populations, or racial minorities, as likely to be guilty of pride as are those who wield power over them? Such questions challenged the prevailing picture of "man" as the subject and began to raise further questions about male superiority, racial and ethnic prejudice, and in general, assumptions about what we value in human beings and in society. I will return to the question of sin below.

So, do we begin theological reflection on our humanity with the assumption that we all share some "essence" of being human, such as our capacity to reason, or our finitude, or, more darkly, our desire for power? Or do we begin with the rich diversity of human lives in our cultures, sexualities, values, and artistic accomplishments? Daniel Horan argues, following the late medieval theologian Duns Scotus, for the latter. God's love for us, he notes, is not a generalized love—think of the *Peanuts* character Charlie Brown's comment that "I love mankind; it's people I can't stand!"—but rather a love for our very uniqueness, our particularity, our "thisness." Only by first recognizing this deeply intimate love of God for us *as who we are uniquely* can we then begin to talk about what it is we share as humans.

The essays in this collection raise these and further questions about what it means to be human. Take for example, the common traditional reference to the supposedly generic "man" as the subject of this area. Not only is male gender assumed, but the person one imagines is usually singular, responsible to himself and to God. But none of us comes into the world or comes to maturity without the care of others amid a complex nexus of relationships. Our *interdependence* with other human beings, with the natural world, with the entire cosmos may be assumed, but is often not valued or even acknowledged. Sometimes it may even be seen as a sign of weakness. So, while there is a need to acknowledge our *autonomy*—that is, the ability to determine the course of our lives and the actions we take—it is just as important to pay attention to our capacity to love, to be vulnerable, to connect in our *relationships*, not only with those in our immediate circle, but also with those in our community, our nation, and in the natural world. This is a point stressed by each of the authors, in different ways. And the *language and images* that we use to talk about relationships are similarly crucial. How do we envisage ourselves and our most intimate connections with others?

The Roman Catholic tradition has historically relied on *natural law*, which basically says that "man" uses "his" rationality to understand God's will as it is manifested in creation. One famous saying is that "grace builds on nature and does not replace it," meaning that we should trust the knowledge we gain from careful observation of the world; God does not work with us apart from the world. Such an understanding values our embodiment and, significantly, also turns to scientific knowledge to explain or expand on what "nature" can teach us. Importantly, the natural world does not dictate any one model or course of action; we must reflect, intelligently and sensitively, on the meaning of what we observe and understand. And while natural law has frequently been challenged or even blamed for overly rigid ideas of human morality, Craig Ford argues that the very fact that we come to know God and learn about God *through our embodied selves* suggests that natural law can be a helpful resource if we use the best science available to us, draw on our lived experiences, and reflect carefully on what we come to learn.

These ideas have had a strong impact especially on theologies of sexuality. Todd Salzman and Michael Lawler take issue with the teaching that our sexual relationships are determined by our biological genitalia—that is, that the only legitimate sexual relationships are heterosexual, and that sexual intercourse is primarily for procreation. They argue instead for a holistic vision of the person in which our entire being—body, spirit, personality—is the subject of the relationship, not just our biology. They call this *holistic complementarity* rather than *genital complementarity*. Similarly, Tina Beattie and Michelle Gonzalez Maldonado question the *images* that we use to describe our relationships with each other and with God. Drawing on the work of Sor Juana Inés de la Cruz, a seventeenth-century Mexican poet and theologian, Gonzalez Maldonado asks us to consider the mostly overlooked areas of women's lives, such as cooking, or those activities deemed lesser than theology, such as poetry. These activities allow us to see the beauty of the world, which in turn expands our ideas of what it means to be human. Beattie is also critical of the ways that the term *woman* has been used in the tradition, and more recently by Pope Francis. Beattie turns to the Trinity as manifesting our inherent relationality; we are in the image of God through our relationships, as God is triune. The abstract and idealistic language used for women by church officials, including Pope Francis and others, Beattie claims, shows their lack of knowledge of what women's and men's lives actually look like. As she puts it, we need "a fully-fleshed account of the human as male and female made in the image of the Trinity."

While theological anthropology has often looked to the spiritual dimension of humanity as the best way to understand our being created in the image of God—think "immortal souls" and bodies as "dust to dust"—M. Shawn Copeland calls out the "false universality" that overlooks or even refuses to see our fleshliness, the particularities of our embodiment. We are all "marked," she argues, with the distinctiveness of our physicality. We are often classified by skin color, height, or differently abled. Some of these marks are "absolutized" and seen as superior to other marks; examples would be race, sexuality, ability. These "marks" need to be acknowledged and valued. Copeland raises up the vulnerability of so many, including Jesus, who have suffered at the hands of others, and says that "the body of the Jewish Jesus, the Christ of God, is the only body capable of taking us all in as we are with all our different body marks."

Along similar lines, Hosffman Ospino raises up the unique experiences of Hispanic/Latiné people. Although Hispanic people were in the Americas years before White colonization, the increased "Browning" of America has raised tensions that have resulted in increasing violence against Hispanic/Latiné people, both long-time and newer residents. Ospino advocates for greater attention to the preferential option for the poor and a recognition of the gifts that the Hispanic/Latiné people bring to understanding humanity, especially our familial and communal connections.

While theological anthropology has mostly focused on the uniqueness of human beings, Elizabeth Johnson and Ilia Delio both insist that we turn our attention to *all* living creatures, and indeed the whole ecosphere. As Johnson notes, "the scope of the world is bigger than us." Pope Francis has made the point repeatedly that "everything is connected," especially in *Laudato Si'*; Johnson looks toward the skies and to the most insignificant creatures (mayflies!) as evidence of God's all-encompassing love and links this to the incarnation, in which God takes on human flesh and dies in solidarity with us. "In their suffering and dying, creatures are not alone." Along the same lines, Ilia Delio emphasizes the complexity and unfinished nature of our existence. Stressing the ongoing dynamic of evolution, Delio highlights our capacity to reflect on ourselves and our relationships, but she especially wants to make clear that we as human beings are part of a much larger and continuing process. Our refusal to be fully a part of this process is what she identifies as sin.

In these essays, sin in some of its most lethal dimensions has already been named: racism, sexism, the destruction of our environment, war, genocide. The unfortunately multiple ways that human beings sin cannot escape our notice. So, is it still possible to talk about "original sin," something every one of us shares in? While *pride* may not be the most appropriate language for the ways that we inevitably fail ourselves, those close to us, and the world around us, are there other ways that can encompass *both* the universality *and* the diversity of sinful human experiences? One possibility has already been named by Ilia Delio: refusal. We can refuse to accept God's love, we can refuse to acknowledge our differences as well as our similarities, we can refuse relationship, we can refuse the implications of our embodiment. The "flip side" of refusal would be openness, acceptance, humility. The contemplative theologian Richard Rohr looks at Alcoholics Anonymous's Twelve Steps as offering clues to understanding our situation as fallible and frail. Refusal to admit the "first step"—that our lives had become unmanageable—is akin to refusing God's love, the love of others, our own limitations, the justice that Jesus called for in his life and teaching.

Living humanly in the way of Christ is our ongoing responsibility. We are challenged to reflect thoughtfully and sensitively on the many ways in which we live, and how we relate to ourselves, others, and God. These essays open up new conversations about our diverse and shared humanity. As the church moves forward in synodality, may we be aware of both our distinctiveness *and* our commonalities and use them in the service of the gospel.

Susan A. Ross

PREFACE

Who are we? How has our understanding of the meaning of being human evolved over time? In twenty-first century cultures, most of us spend the majority of our time engaged in diverse acts of survival. As adults we think or worry about our finances, relationships, work, and how to manage these. Along the way we confuse what we do with who we are, and eventually we neglect to wonder who we are in relation to God.

Or perhaps you think about this identity question often, and maybe a rote answer from the *Catechism* comes to mind: "God made us to show forth His goodness and to share with us His everlasting happiness in heaven." Or maybe something more altruistic feels right: you seek to find your true self in serving others.

While these reflections may be a good start, they are only a beginning, because the world, the Church, and our understanding of what it means to be a human being have changed dramatically in the last hundred years. To attend to these changes Pope Francis called for a Global Synod on Synodality in 2021, to listen to the joys and concerns of the whole people of God. In 2023, the assembly of the Synod of Bishops in Rome invited the entire Church to think together about the meaning of our existence in relationship with God and with each other. They emphasized that in order to be up to the challenges of contemporary life, our religious understandings of ourselves—our theological anthropologies—must "grasp the complexity of the elements emerging from experience or knowledge in the sciences" (III.15.g) including the "bodiliness" (III.15.g) of our sexuality, our gender, and our interdependence with the rest of creation, and "[integrate] them into a more mature synthesis" (III.14.h).

In response to this challenge, we asked prominent scholars to share their thoughts on these questions. In the spirit of the ongoing dialogue in our synodal church, we share their essays with you, and invite you to ponder, discern, and reflect with others on the meaning of being human.

May the blessings of our loving God be with you in your discernment.

Elsie M. Miranda
Director of Diversities
The Association of Theological Schools

Cristina L. H. Traina
Avery Cardinal Dulles, SJ,
Professor of Catholic Theology
Fordham University

ACKNOWLEDGMENTS

As the last edits for this book were being submitted, we came to the realization that much gratitude needed to be expressed across various sectors of what we know to *be* the Church. First and foremost, we wish to offer a word of gratitude to the Holy Father, Pope Francis, who at the close of the XV General Assembly of the Synod, 2023, explicitly encouraged Catholic theologians to propose new theological anthropologies for our time.

This invitation led us to wonder, "Who is going to take up that task, and how might the wisdom that has already been put forth by Catholic theologians be raised up to inform the Synod, and the scattered Catholics in our local communities?" Within the next few hours, we found ourselves, like St. Francis before the cross of San Damiano, hearing in our heart of hearts—I choose *you*...! The very next day we came up with a short list of colleagues whom we invited to write short essays, addressing new theological anthropologies for our time. Our objective was to share these with Pope Francis, members of the Synodal assembly, and eventually with a broader Catholic audience.

As if orchestrated by the Holy Spirit herself, everyone we invited to contribute said yes! We are both eternally grateful for the trust, faithfulness, and generosity of all of the contributors to this project: Tina Beattie, M. Shawn Copeland, Ilia Delio, Craig Ford, Michelle

Gonzalez-Maldonado, Daniel Horan, Elizabeth Johnson, Hosffman Ospino, Susan A. Ross, Todd Salzman and Michael Lawler. This has been an exciting and Spirit-led initiative that has expanded the meaning of being human beyond the Aristotelian notion of the superior and godly rational man to include the particularity of other forms of embodiment as equal in dignity and value. We look forward to the emerging fruits of the conversations these essays and webinars will engender.

In keeping with this movement of the Spirit, we are also grateful to Father René Constanza, CSP, and Paul McMahon of Paulist Press, who expressed their enthusiasm for publishing this book, and to Daniel Horan and the Center for the Study of Spirituality at Saint Mary's College for hosting our initial webinar series. The ease of producing this little book can only be attributed to the grace of God, working through the many good and faith-filled servants who have shared wisdom and have been companions on this journey.

As we join in synodal solidarity with Catholics around the world, we share this work with you in the hopes that it continues to breathe a life of its own, and that it informs, inspires, and serves to accompany others on their journey toward a more globally interconnected world where we all belong in the fullness of our humanity, as children of the living God.

"THE MEANING OF BEING HUMAN" SERIES RECORDINGS

Webinar 1:
https://youtu.be/4AVIZ0B3uHc?si=1X7MWwCw7eVBEvck

Webinar 2:
https://youtu.be/Zp4d51yJfIY?si=tb27NUZNQ5SbGEEY

Webinar 3:
https://youtu.be/Jj027A0ERKc?si=SnrP7VNnHmtWd9Yw

For more information about upcoming events at the Center for the Study of Spirituality, visit https://www.saintmarys.edu/spiritual-life/center-for-spirituality/events.

1
EVOLUTION TOWARD PERSONHOOD

Ilia Delio, OSF

One of the most beautiful accounts of the Book of Genesis is the opening page, which describes the beginning of creation by God. The author writes that the earth was an empty and formless void, darkness covered the deep, and the Spirit hovered over the waters. Then God spoke and said, "Let there be light!" The creation story begins with the Spirit of God, forming earthly life out of chaos, culminating in the creation of the human person as image of God. This story has been told through the ages, engraved in the religious imagination of Christians. When Charles Darwin, in the nineteenth century, suggested the term *evolution* to describe the variety of species by means of natural selection, he had no idea that he sparked one of the most significant paradigm shifts of the modern age. His theory put him at odds with the monotheistic religions because evolution seemed to dispense with need for a Creator. Today we are realizing that evolution provides a rich context for the deep relationship between the human person and the natural world and impels us to reconsider the God-world relationship.

Evolution is not a background to the human story; it *is* the human story. The Jesuit scientist Pierre Teilhard de Chardin described evolution as a progression toward more unified matter and consciousness. He linked evolution of the mind with physical and mental energy, which are corelated in the evolutionary movement. Matter is the matrix of consciousness, he wrote, and spirit is the higher portion of matter. Life is oriented toward spirit and hence toward Absolute Spirit or God. The human person is integrally part of evolution, in that we rise from the process; however, in reflecting on the process we stand apart from it. Teilhard defined reflection as "the power acquired by consciousness to turn in upon itself, to take possession of itself *as an object*...no longer merely to know, but to know that we know."[1] The human person is "the point of emergence in nature at which this deep cosmic evolution culminates and declares itself";[2] that is, we are the level of evolution at which thought is born.

To realize that humans are part of a larger process that involves long spans of developmental time brings a massive change to all our knowledge and beliefs. Evolution might lead us to think that the human person is mere animal, not image of God. However, Teilhard did not see the human person lost or insignificant because of evolution. Rather, he saw the human person as one truly unique, not a chance arrival but an integral element of the physical world, gradually forming from the organic nutrients of earthly life. This idea was affirmed by Karl Rahner, who advocated a deeper and more comprehensive "pancosmic" relationship to the material universe. Rahner drew from the German philosopher Martin Heidegger the notion that one can never separate the human from the world. To be human is to be in the world, indeed, it is to be precisely that part of the world that questions. As Rahner put it, "Human beings are bodily creatures who have a fundamentally unlimited openness to being as such in knowledge and freedom."[3] Theologian Philip Hefner identifies the human person as "created co-creator," which is a symbol for understanding ourselves in the evolutionary story. Human evolution, from Big Bang to the present time, emphasizes our oneness with the creation and our belongingness to those processes that have brought us into being. We are the creative edge of evolution through our capacity to think and imagine. This picture makes a difference in how we understand human evolution for several reasons. First, it puts our giftedness as humans, our extraordinary brains and our self-awareness, our language and symbol using, within the evolutionary process itself. We are not the great exception to nature, nor are we set apart over nature or superior to it. Rather, we are a development of natural trajectories of evolution. Second, this drama of evolution describes our vocation, our calling within the creation—that is, to use our gifts of mind, imagination, and creative spirit to be part of nature's ongoing development, in cooperation with God. As Hefner states, "We do not transcend nature; *nature transcends itself in us*."[4] Our gifts are intended to play a role in and for the natural order. Being human involves creating and imagining new worlds and constructing those worlds. Co-creating is not just our doing; it is our being. In Teilhard's terms, we humans do not work for ourselves, but it is the creation, evolution, working within us and through us. We are brought into relationship by the fact that we are created, and we create on behalf of that which has created us.

Paul Tillich spoke of the multidimensional unity of life, incorporating in humans the evolved constellation of a number of dimensions, which he names the inorganic, the organic, the animal, the self-aware, the psychological, and the spiritual. To be a person is to engage in the struggle to center this vast array of conditioning material so as to form a coherent self. Personal identity is shaped by one's embodied and historical engagement with the material world in the ongoing creation of the spirit to form a coherent self. The soul is not extrinsic to the emergence of the human person but an intrinsic part of the self's ongoing constitutive core relationships.

Human personhood is marked by intrinsic relatedness because we are created in the image of the triune God and oriented to God through our relationships with the natural world and with one another. Although original sin as a universal condition has been challenged, if not outrightly rejected by some scholars in light of evolution, the ongoing emergence of personhood undergirds the human person *in fieri* (in process, becoming) and hence oriented toward completion. In a universe still coming into existence, and in a biological process of evolution open to greater complexity, the human person is unfinished. Sin can be seen as the condition of resistance to greater wholeness or completion, choosing against relationships of evolution toward more being and consciousness. If the direction of evolution is toward more life up ahead, sin is the rejection of a new future, that is, the rejection of more life together.

Teilhard identified an irresistible presence within evolution not subject to the laws of entropy, a wholeness that continues to shape evolution and give it its form of personalization. He identified this presence as Omega, a centrating principle *within* evolution that emerges more coherently with increased complexity and consciousness.

He identified Omega with love and the energetic presence of divine love. God is within, emerging through the rise of consciousness and seeking to be actualized in love; yet God is also ahead as the power of the future. In this respect, the future is constantly arriving, as love is actualized in evolution.

Historian David Noble suggested that the drive toward God undergirds the development of artificial intelligence. We seek perfectibility and unlimited knowledge, he claims, because we are driven by being *imago Dei*. Without a fuller and coherent story of the human person in evolution, mind, matter, and spirit are disjointed, leaving a yawning gap between nature and person, a gap that artificial intelligence aims to fill with ideals of superintelligence and transcendence of biological limits. Teilhard postulated that evolution is impelled by the irresistible love of Omega and that computer technology can support creative evolution toward Omega by drawing individual minds and hearts into a complexified whole. The success of computer technology, however, depends on how we control our psychic, spiritual energy needs and powers. Computers may enhance the convergence of networked minds, but love draws us onward to more life. Thought can lead us to new horizons of insight but love alone can bring us to another universe.

REFLECTION QUESTIONS

1. Are you aware of being in the dynamic flow of evolution? How does this awareness influence your experience of self and God? Your relationship with the world?

2. The openness of the human person to more life suggests that the human person is unfinished or incomplete. Can we think of sin as incompleteness?
3. How can we understand our role in evolution as cocreators in a way that nurtures our integral relationship to the natural world?
4. What does this statement mean to you? "We do not transcend nature; nature transcends itself in us."

SUGGESTED READING

Doming, Daryl P., and Monika Hellwig. *Original Selfishness: Original Sin and Evil in Light of Evolution*. New York: Routledge, 2006.

Haught, John. *The Cosmic Vision of Teilhard de Chardin*. Maryknoll, NY: Orbis Books, 2021.

Hefner, Philip. "The Human Person as *Imago Dei*." In *The Human Person in Science and Theology*, edited by Niels Henrik Gregersen, Willem Drees, and Ulf Görman. Edinburgh: T&T Clark, 2000.

———. "A Fuller Concept of Evolution—Big Bang to Spirit." *Zygon* 47, no. 2 (2012): 298–307.

Noble, David. *The Religion of Technology: The Divinity of Man and the Spirit of Invention*. New York: Knopf, 1997.

Rahner, Karl. "Natural Science and Reasonable Faith: Theological Perspectives for Dialogue with the Natural Sciences." In *Theological Investigations* XXI, translated by Hugh M. Riley. New York: Crossroad, 1988.

Teilhard de Chardin, Pierre. *Human Energy*. Translated by J. M. Cohen. New York: Harcourt Brace Jovanovich, 1969.

———. *The Human Phenomenon*. Translated by Sarah Appleton-Weber. Brighton, UK: Sussex Academic Press, 1999.

Notes

1. Pierre Teilhard de Chardin, *The Human Phenomenon*, trans. Sarah Appleton-Weber (Brighton, UK: Sussex Academic Press, 1999), 110.

2. Pierre Teilhard de Chardin, *Human Energy*, trans. J. M. Cohen (New York: Harcourt Brace Jovanovich, 1969), 23.

3. Karl Rahner, "Natural Science and Reasonable Faith: Theological Perspectives for Dialogue with the Natural Sciences," in *Theological Investigations* XXI, trans. Hugh M. Riley (New York: Crossroad, 1988), 42.

4. Philip Hefner, "A Fuller Concept of Evolution—Big Bang to Spirit," *Zygon* 47, no. 2 (2012): 304.

2
HUMAN BEINGS
Redeemed with the Community of Creation

Elizabeth A. Johnson, CSJ

The view of Earth from space has become commonplace but still its wonder remains fresh. There we spin, a beautiful blue marble swaddled with white clouds, luminous against endless dark space. Unique in the solar system, the planet teems with life. Its land, waters, and air host a dazzling array of creatures from tiny ants to giant sequoias, from eagles to whales, from kangaroos to human beings.

This distant view makes it crystal clear that human beings belong to a world larger than themselves. We belong to an interconnected world with relationships pulsing in every direction. The traditions of indigenous peoples everywhere are rich with this insight. Scripture, too, begins with the story of God creating a whole world that is "very good," and ends with a hopeful vision of all creation being redeemed.

Until recently we in Western culture mostly defined ourselves apart from this broader world. Influential philosophies, cultural forces, and business practices modeled the world as a pyramid with humans dominating from the pinnacle, rather than as a circle of kinship with humans in an interconnected, responsible position. We have defined ourselves "above" other creatures as their lords and masters, with devastating results.

Going counter to this view of isolated human supremacy, Pope Francis's encyclical *Laudato Si': On Care for Our Common Home* (*LS*) aims to heal our broken sense of community. In tune with scripture, it teaches that human beings are not the only recipients of God's love. Rather, the love of God is the origin, sustaining power, and goal of the whole shebang. "God's love is the fundamental moving force in all created things," writes the pope; "even the fleeting life of the least of beings is the object of God's love, and in its few seconds of existence, God enfolds it with affection" (*LS* 77). Commentators note that here Francis had in mind mayflies. After hatching these little insects live for only a few hours, during which they must find a matc and lay eggs; then they die. So ephemeral. But enfolded with affection. As are we all. Creation means that we humans "are not disconnected from the rest of creatures but joined together in a splendid universal communion" (*LS* 220).

It is one of the blessings of our era that scientific study reaches a similar conclusion by its own distinctive methods. Biologically, all living species evolved from common ancestors in the ancient seas and share a deep genetic history. Charles Darwin makes the point with flair: "What can be more curious than that the hand of a man formed for grasping, that of a mole for digging, the leg of the horse, the paddle of the porpoise, and the wing of the bat, should all be constructed on the same pattern, and should include the same bones, in the same relative positions?"[1] The reason, he explains, is that an ancient progenitor had its limbs arranged this way and all descendants inherit the pattern. Over time the bones might be enveloped in a thick membrane to form a paddle to swim, or a thin membrane to form a wing, or they might be separated to form fingers and toes, but there will be no tendency to alter the framework.

Rather than being sealed up tight, our human bodies have open borders. We evolved from a developing line of mammals and our very existence depends on interaction with the rest of the natural world.

Chemically, too, we are connected to the cosmos. Life on Earth evolved using elements from the planet, which is part of the solar system, which formed out of the dust and gas of older exploding stars in our Milky Way galaxy. Why is our blood and the blood of most other animals red? Because of hemoglobin, which contains iron and, as one scientist observed, "every atom of iron in our blood would not be there had it not been produced in some galactic explosion billions of years ago and eventually condensed to form the iron in the crust of the earth from which we have emerged."

According to science as well as theology there is but one community of life on Earth. Science calls it the biosphere. Theology calls it the community of creation. The landscape of our imagination expands when we realize that our human connection to the natural world is so deep that we can no longer adequately define our human identity without including our shared history with other species and with the cosmos itself. This strengthens the realization that humans are kin with the bear, the squid, the raven, and the bugs, all created by the generous love of the living God. In this light the incarnation of Jesus Christ, his life, death, and resurrection, bring the good news of salvation not only for human beings but for the whole creation.

Start with the incarnation. "The Word became flesh and lived among us," testifies John's Gospel (John 1:14 NRSV). What is this flesh? It is the material of the world, beautiful but prone to decay. The phrase "deep incarnation" is starting to be used as shorthand that signifies a radical divine reach through human flesh in Jesus Christ into the very matrix of biological existence itself. Born of a woman, the Word of God became a creature of Earth. The genes of his body were kin to the flowers, frogs, fish, finches, foxes, the whole evolving community of life. By joining human flesh, Christ is connected not only to human beings but also to the whole biological world of living creatures and the cosmic dust of which they are composed.

Trace the significance of this insight into Jesus's death and resurrection. All creatures come to an end; those with nervous systems know pain and suffering. Jesus's anguished suffering and death on the cross place him in solidarity with this company. It is as if by inhabiting the inside of the isolating shell of death Christ crucified brings divine life into closest contact with disaster, setting up a gleam of light for all others who suffer that same annihilating suffocation. In their suffering and dying, creatures are not alone. God, who is love, is with them amid the shocking enormity of pain and death, there, in the godforsaken moment, as only the giver of life can be, with the promise of something more.

Joyful Alleluias ring out at Easter celebrating that Jesus died not into nothingness but into the loving embrace of God, who raised him with affection into new transfigured life. Given his solidarity with the flesh, this destiny signals a blessed future for all human beings, but not only for us. Christ is "the firstborn of all creation," we read in scripture (Col 1:15 NRSV). "In Christ's resurrection the earth itself arose," preached the fourth-century bishop Ambrose. While this is hardly imaginable, it is not wishful thinking. It bears the logic of belief in God that does not stop halfway but follows the road consistently to the end, trusting that the Alpha who uttered the first word is also the Omega who will have the last word, and it is the same loving word: "Let there be life."

In life Jesus was part of the community of creation; in death he is in solidarity with all who die; in resurrected life he anchors hope for the whole world. Although we humans have been inclined to separate ourselves from other species, Earth and its inhabitants are created by the same generous God. All share in the identity of being beloved creatures. For all our human difference, this shared identity makes us kin with the land, sea, and sky, and with the horse, the salmon, the crow, the bee, the olive tree, and the stars in one grand community of creation destined for joy.

REFLECTION QUESTIONS

1. What is the benefit of placing human beings in a circle of kinship? How does that shift impact our sense of human identity as well as the dynamics of power between human beings and the rest of Earth's creatures?
2. How does widening Jesus's relation to the flesh of Earth affect your own relationship to Christ?

3. What ethical responsibility toward the Earth and all its species, including human beings, flows from this theological approach?

SUGGESTED READING

Bauckham, Richard. *The Bible and Ecology: Rediscovering the Community of Creation*. Waco, TX: Baylor University Press, 2010.

Edwards, Denis. *Ecology at the Heart of Faith*. Maryknoll, NY: Orbis Books, 2006.

Fiand, Barbara. *Awe-Filled Wonder: The Interface of Science and Spirituality*. Mahwah, NJ: Paulist Press, 2008.

Francis, Pope. *Laudato Si': On Care for Our Common Home*. Vatican City, 2015. Referred to in the text as *LS*.

Johnson, Elizabeth. *Come, Have Breakfast: Meditations on God and the Earth*. Maryknoll, NY: Orbis Books, 2024.

———. "Jesus and the Earth," in Johnson, *Come, Have Breakfast*, 91–144.

———. "Humankind and Otherkind," in Johnson, *Come, Have Breakfast*, 147–76.

Kimmerer, Robin Wall. *Braiding Sweetgrass: Indigenous Wisdom, Scientific Knowledge, and the Teachings of Plants*. Minneapolis: Milkweed Editions, 2013.

Nash, James. *Loving Nature: Ecological Integrity and Christian Responsibility*. Nashville: Abingdon Press, 1991.

Notes

1. Charles Darwin, *On the Origin of Species* (New York: Barnes and Noble Classics, 2004), 343.

3

GOD CREATES THE PARTICULAR

Human Dignity and Diversity in Theological Anthropology

Daniel P. Horan

When God creates, does God first envision something generic and universal or individual and particular? For example, considering all the billions or trillions of blades of grass that grow on this planet, each created by and sustained in existence by God, what comes first in the divine creative act: Is it the idea of "grass" in general or *this* particular blade of grass? The same question could be posed about any other creature in the universe. And the same question applies to humanity.

For many centuries, the most popular conception of how God creates starts with the species or genus of something: this *kind* of plant, this *kind* of animal, this *kind* of creature. One way that philosophers and theologians have described this manner of thinking has been to talk about the "common nature" of a certain set of creatures—like humans or dogs or trees—that prioritizes what is seen as shared among the individuals in that set. What comes first, in other words, is the abstracted nature or essence of a thing. In Latin this is known as the *quidditas* (the "whatness") and when it comes to God's creative act, many theologians in the Middle Ages and later emphasized that this *quid* or "what" is prior to the individual or specific person, place, or thing.

Therefore, according to this view, when God decides to create, God first conceives of the essence or *quidditas* and then only secondarily "individuates" or makes something particular from what is first shared in common. According to thinkers like the Dominican theologian Thomas Aquinas (d. 1274), who was influenced by the ancient philosophical worldview of Aristotle (d. 322 BCE), the thing that makes something an individual is a distinctive set of "attributes" or "properties," what we might call details, that distinguish an individual within the group. To put it simply, God first decides to create "trees" and then differentiates *this* tree from *that* tree according to its location, height, color, shape, and so forth. What is most important is its tree-ness (*quidditas*) and only secondarily is its particular identity as an individual tree important.

There are many reasons why this way of thinking about what medieval scholars referred to as the relationship between "universals" and "particulars" makes sense. It certainly seems efficient, especially from our vantage point where, as humans, we have limited time and intellectual capacity. But such a way of thinking about how God creates can also lead to problems, not the least of which is the assumed priority and importance of what is believed to be held in common or the "what" (*quid*) of something over the actual, specific, particular person or thing itself.

Practically speaking, in order to group creatures into such categories organized by a presumed "common nature," someone has to establish criteria to delimit who or what is in or out, what does or does not "make the cut" in terms of qualifying for membership within a certain "common nature" according to *quidditas*. While maybe not intentional, this way of thinking can lead to exclusionary and discriminatory practices when a person or thing is determined to not (or no longer) meet the standards or criteria for inclusion in the "common nature." And in the case of human persons, this can result in dehumanization and sometimes violence.

But there are other ways to think about how God creates that do not give precedence to the abstracted essence or "common nature" of a set of creatures. One example comes to us from the medieval Franciscan theologian and philosopher John Duns Scotus (d. 1308). Although Scotus was also influenced by Aristotle, he had a radically different view about God's creative act and intention. Rather than beginning with the generic essence, nature, or *quidditas* ("whatness") of a person or thing, Scotus argued that God created by first envisioning the particular or individual, giving priority not to the *quidditas* but to the *haecceitas* ("thisness"). The dignity and value of creation is not grounded in one's alignment or conformity to an abstracted idea or essence, but instead is rooted in the very particularity of an individual—each and every person or thing's *this-ness*.

Scotus absolutely believed in something like a "common nature," but he recognized that it is secondary to the particular. He argued that the condition of the possibility for even recognizing that which is common among individuals was first knowing a range of particulars and deducing what is shared among them. We know the category or essence of "horse-ness" not because we first encounter the abstracted nature of "horse," but because we encounter *this* horse and *that* horse and Lassie, which is actually a dog and not a horse at all. We only ever experience particulars in reality and not abstractions, which helps shed light on why Scotus insisted on the primacy of the particular while also affirming the reality of commonality. He believed that there was something true that is shared among those who belong to what we can call a "common nature," but that isn't what comes first for God.

Instead, God *loves* each and every aspect of creation into existence, knows each creature *specifically* and not merely abstractly. According to Scotus, God knows every blade of grass and grain of sand and human person that has ever lived on this planet. Not only does God know and love these creatures into existence, but because God envisions their particularity—their *haecceity*—and then loves this particular creature into being, one's dignity and value is not tied to conformity to an abstract type but is irrevocably tied to who we are in the truest, deepest, most personal sense as known by God.

Diversity, then, is not a problem according to this understanding for the foundation of theological anthropology. God creates the particular, knows the particular, loves the particular. And when it comes to human creatures specifically, God loves us in all our glorious individuality, because God intended humanity to be a community of persons existing in mutual and right relationship.

According to Scotus, what makes us who we are is this divinely designed and gifted *haecceitas*, which is unique to each creature. Our *haecceitas* is inalienable and unrepeatable, which means that it can never be taken away nor will anyone else ever inhabit it. Put simply, each human person is indeed one of a kind! In fact, Scotus believes this applies not just to humans, but also to all of creation, which means each snowflake is indeed unique, each blade of grass, each grain of sand, and each dog or cat we encounter. There has never been one like you before and there will never be another you again.

This notion of God loving us *particularly* and *individually* into existence is not simply a philosophical or theological concept, but it also finds resonance in scripture, such as in the Book of Jeremiah when God proclaims, "Before I formed you in the womb I knew you" (1:5 NRSV), or Psalm 139:14 (NRSV), which reads, "I praise you, for I am fearfully and wonderfully made." Or, think about the intimacy and familiarity with which God knows each of us as Jesus explains in the Gospel of Luke: "But even the hairs of your head are all counted" (12:7 NRSV).

So impactful has Scotus's way of thinking about creation and creaturely identity been over the centuries that some of the most inspiring spiritual writers and poets have popularized it. The great Jesuit poet Gerard Manley Hopkins (d. 1889) coined the term *inscape* drawing on Scotus's *haecceitas*, which inspired his poem "As Kingfishers Catch Fire." The Trappist monk, mystic, and spiritual writer Thomas Merton developed his notion of the "True Self," which is developed in his writings such as *New Seeds of Contemplation*.

For as much as Scotus's foundational thought on the dignity and value of the human person specifically and the whole of creation generally shaped the theological and spiritual thinking and works of renowned authors like Hopkins and Merton, it has received little attention by the majority of Christians and Church leaders. All of our Church documents that address human personhood presuppose a version of the Thomistic emphasis on *quidditas* as an essential part of its operative theological anthropology. This explains why there are some tensions that exist in the current presentation of teaching on issues related to human dignity, sexuality, and gender, among other topics. However, the case of Scotus's thought demonstrates that there are other ways of thinking and understanding the human person, especially when considering the infinite range of diversity among humanity. What might our theological and ethical worldview look like if we started not with what was presupposed to be universal, but recognized instead the divinely intended particulars reflected in each individual's *haecceitas* loved into existence by God?

REFLECTION QUESTIONS

1. When I think about God creating all that inhabits this universe, including me, how do I envision God's creative act?
2. What is appealing and what is challenging about starting with the particular when thinking about human dignity and value?
3. How might our theological imaginations, pastoral practices, and personal relationships be changed by renewing our understanding of God's knowing and loving the particular into existence?

SUGGESTED READING

Hopkins, Gerard Manley. *Poems and Prose*. Edited by W. H. Gardner. Harmondsworth, Middlesex: Penguin Classics, 1985.

Horan, Daniel P. *Catholicity and Emerging Personhood: A Contemporary Theological Anthropology*. Maryknoll, NY: Orbis Books, 2019.

———. *The Franciscan Heart of Thomas Merton: A New Look at the Spiritual Influence of His Life, Thought, and Writing*. Notre Dame, IN: Ave Maria Press, 2014.

Ingham, Mary Beth. *Scotus for Dunces: An Introduction to the Subtle Doctor*. St. Bonaventure, NY: Franciscan Institute Publications, 2003.

———. *Understanding John Duns Scotus*. St. Bonaventure, NY: Franciscan Institute Publications, 2017.

Merton, Thomas. *New Seeds of Contemplation*. New York: New Directions, 1961.

4
THEOLOGICAL ANTHROPOLOGY AND WOMEN'S LIVES

Tina Beattie

"Woman, what have you to do with me?"
John 2:4 RSV

Pope Francis is restoring to Catholic teaching a rich creation-centered theology, focusing on the significance of the Trinity for our understanding of the intrinsic relationality of all forms of life. This cosmic trinitarian vision is not new to the Catholic tradition—it can be found in much patristic and medieval theology—but it has been neglected through what he calls the "excessive anthropocentrism" of modernity. This has given rise to "a wrong understanding of the relationship between human beings and the world" (*Laudato Si'* 116). Referring to Saint Bonaventure, Pope Francis writes that "for Christians, believing in one God who is trinitarian communion suggests that the Trinity has left its mark on all creation." This challenges us to try to "read reality in a Trinitarian key" because "the world, created according to the divine model, is a web of relationships....Everything is interconnected, and this invites us to develop a spirituality of that global solidarity which flows from the mystery of the Trinity" (*LS* 240).

This relational theology has profound anthropological implications. Feminist thinkers argue that Christian anthropology has been shaped by Greek philosophical concepts of the divine, so that masculinity is associated with form, rationality, transcendence, independence, and activity, and femininity is associated with matter, emotion, dependence, immanence, and passivity. This gives rise to a theology that is far removed from the biblical understanding of a God who accompanies humankind through history, who is revealed in and speaks through the natural world, and who in the incarnation enters fully into the human condition to redeem creation from within. To quote Pope Francis: "He comes not from above but from within, he comes that we might find him in this world of ours" (*LS* 236).

This incarnational trinitarian theology constitutes a paradigm shift in the language of modern Church teaching. It has the potential to usher in a transformation in what it means to be made in the image of God, not as the autonomous masculine subject modeled on the God of philosophical theism, but as an interdependent bodily self whose identity is constituted not by individuality but by relationality. Thomas Aquinas argues that the persons of the Trinity derive their identities from their relationships to one another, so that, even though all our language falls short when we speak of the divine mystery, the closest we can come to expressing the reality of God is in the language of relations (*ST* I, 28, 1).

Also relevant to this question of anthropology is

Pope Francis's emphasis on the significance of culture and history for incarnating the Christian faith in diverse contexts. He writes that "the People of God is incarnate in the peoples of the earth, each of which has its own culture....It has to do with the lifestyle of a given society, the specific way in which its members relate to one another, to other creatures and to God" (*Evangelii Gaudium* 115).

This is an invitation to develop a Christian anthropology that weaves together the universality of what it means to be a human person made in the image of the trinitarian, interpersonal God, and an understanding of how to interpret this in lives incarnated in particular cultures and communities. It calls for reflection on how our relationships with one another and with our environments and habitats shape our senses of self and others, as interdependent creatures in God's very good creation. It allows for the accommodation of different forms of expression and models of relationality, through a diverse and multifaceted understanding of the Catholic tradition as many traditions nesting within the core doctrinal mysteries and sacramental practices of our shared faith.

But when we look at the ways in which the language of "woman" is used in official Church documents, we discover that many of these principles are ignored. "Woman" is an abstract and idealized concept that bears little relationship to the incarnational realities of women's lives. Pope Francis repeatedly refers to the Church as a woman, which suggests that the idea of woman floats free of any necessary relationship to the female body. In *Laudato Si'*, he represents "Mother Earth" in the language of maternal femininity, without any reference to the substantial contribution that women are making to ecological initiatives in activism and scholarship. The female body has metaphorical significance for ecclesiology and ecology but lacks incarnational meaning as a locus of revelation and living sacramental presence. This undermines any attempts to incorporate reflection on women's lives into Church teaching, which cannot develop an adequate anthropology so long as man is the subject and woman is the silenced and excluded object, spoken about but never permitted to speak.

Pope Francis has made dialogue a central theme of all his teachings, including the need for dialogue that is not afraid of disagreement and struggle, in the quest for what he refers to as a "reconciled diversity" (*EG* 230). There is an urgent need for magisterial dialogue with women theologians, biblical scholars, and philosophers representing a wide range of geographical and socioeconomic contexts, in order to develop a pastorally informed approach to the experiences of women in different cultures and contexts. This calls for an attentive focus on how gender, sexuality, pregnancy, childbirth and motherhood, poverty, environmental destruction, war and violence, domestic and cultural environments, and education and leadership impact upon the lives of women and girls, not in terms of the generalized references we find in some documents, but through engaging with the varied and complex realities of women's lives. This would in turn lead to new ways of understanding how we relate to one another and to our natural environments, as sexed bodies, gendered subjects, and creatures who participate in the trinitarian life of all creation.

The lives of the women saints provide some resources for the construction of a theological anthropology that includes the fullness of sexual difference in its many forms of expression, but these have been filtered and authorized through the lens of an exclusively male celibate hierarchy. Anthropological insights about women's historical lives have to be excavated from often sanitized hagiographies, and from the writings of those women themselves—described as mystics but increasingly recognized as vernacular theologians. Similarly, there is much in Marian theology and devotion that can be reclaimed and reinterpreted, but this too is a challenging task. Modern Mariology has been used to idealize and simultaneously suppress women, rather than call them to the fullness of life. This idealization may be subtle, but its representation of virginal maternal perfection is an impossible model for women to emulate. The meek and obedient Madonna of modern Marian devotion seems far removed from the courage and commitment of the biblical Mary, who sang the Magnificat, accompanied Jesus throughout his earthly ministry, and remained with him as he suffered and died on the cross.

One cannot just add women and stir to compensate for these omissions and distortions. The full incorporation of incarnate female personhood into Church doctrine, sacramentality, ethics, and liturgy would be a catalyst for a transformed vision of what it means to be human. The gendered fluidity of trinitarian language in premodern theology also has much to offer in this respect. The Holy Spirit is often feminized in early Christian writings, the image of Jesus as mother was popular in medieval devotions, and in the seventh century the Council of Toledo described Christ as coming from the womb of the Father (*de utero patris*). There are many resources that would allow for the development of doctrine to accommodate a fully fleshed account of the human as male and female made in the image of the Trinity.

The groundwork for this kind of transformation has been laid in documents such as *Laudato Si'*, but it remains empty of content. Much of what Pope Francis calls for in that encyclical has already been expressed and developed by feminist theologians, including ecofeminists, so that there are deep resonances between his critique of modern anthropology and the feminist theological quest for a more relational, incarnational, and creation-centered theology.

These are constructive opportunities for creative new ways of expressing, living, and exploring the neglected and hidden dimensions of our beautiful but diminished tradition. The Catholic faith is an abundant treasury of incarnate wisdom, but we need to dig deep to recover its buried treasures and unfulfilled promises of redemption, freedom, and flourishing for all God's creatures. This is an exciting and challenging task as we seek to discern a path through the rocky terrain ahead, with so many struggles and sorrows threatening our wounded planet—this glistening blue pearl spinning its path through time and space in the infinite mystery of creation.

Jesus still asks us the same question that he asked of his mother in John's Gospel, "Woman, what have you to do with me?" Only when the Church's official magisterium includes women as full and equal partners in discipleship, leadership, and scholarship, might we begin to respond to that question.

REFLECTION QUESTIONS

1. In what ways do you find your faith challenged or inspired by Pope Francis's trinitarian, creation-centered theology?

2. How has your faith been influenced for better or worse by the Church's teaching on gender and sexual difference?
3. How might your sense of self be changed by the kind of anthropological vision outlined in this reflection?
4 In what ways do you think your culture and material environment shape your faith?

SUGGESTED READING

Beattie, Tina. "Repairing the Sacred Canopy—a Reflection on the Symbolic Anthropology of Church Documents from the Council to *Mulieris Dignitatem*," in *We Have Something to Say: Theologians Re-read Vatican II*, edited by Marinella Perroni and Hervé Legrand. *Saggistica* series. Rome: Edizioni Paoline, 2016.

———. "The Theological Study of Gender." In *The Oxford Handbook of the Study of Theology, Sexuality and Gender*, edited by Adrian Thatcher. Oxford: Oxford University Press, 2014.

Beattie, Tina, and Diana Culbertson, eds. *Catholic Women Speak: Bringing Our Gifts to the Table*. Mahwah NJ: Paulist Press, 2015.

———. *Visions and Vocations*. Mahwah, NJ: Paulist Press, 2018.

Coakley, Sarah. *God, Sexuality, and the Self: An Essay "On the Trinity."* New York: Cambridge University Press, 2013.

Deane-Drummond, Celia. *A Primer in Ecotheology: Theology for a Fragile Earth*. Eugene, OR: Cascade Books, 2017.

Francis, Pope. *Evangelii Gaudium*. November 24, 2013. https://www.vatican.va/content/francesco/en/apost

_exhortations/documents/papa-francesco_esortazione-ap_20131124_evangelii-gaudium.html. Abbreviated in text as *EG*.

———. *Laudato Si'*. May 24, 2015. https://www.vatican.va/content/francesco/en/encyclicals/documents/papa-francesco_20150524_enciclica-laudato-si.html. Abbreviated in text as *LS*.

Graff, Ann O'Hara, ed. *In the Embrace of God: Feminist Approaches to Theological Anthropology*. Maryknoll, NY: Orbis Books, 1995.

Johnson, Elizabeth A. *She Who Is: The Mystery of God in Feminist Theological Discourse*. New York: Crossroad, 1992.

Ruether, Rosemary Radford, ed. *Women Healing Earth: Third World Women on Ecology, Feminism, and Religion*. Maryknoll, NY: Orbis Books, 1996.

Soskice, Janet Martin. "*Imago Dei*." In *The Kindness of God: Metaphor, Gender, and Religious Language*. Oxford: Oxford University Press, 2007.

Thomas Aquinas. *Summa Theologiae*. Abbreviated in text as *ST*.

5
MARKING THE BODY OF CHRIST

M. Shawn Copeland

From its very beginning, Christianity has struggled to understand, interpret, and sustain the startling mystery that the eternal Divine Word, the *Logos,* truly became flesh, became the bodily, concrete, marked, historical Jew Jesus of Nazareth; that Jesus died, rather than betray his mission, his love for God and for human beings; that his fidelity, integrity, and love were vindicated, and his crucified body was raised glorious from the dead. This is the teaching of the doctrine of the incarnation, and this teaching affirms the value and significance of the human body, which must never be degraded, disregarded, or treated with contempt. At the same time, the Christian tradition displays theological ambivalence toward the body. On the one hand, the tradition affirms the goodness of creation, the sacredness of the body; on the other hand, the tradition discounts our bodies, prefers celibate life over marriage, mistrusts bodily pleasures of food, drink, or sex, and associates women with the body and men with the spirit.

While Christian theology acknowledges the significance of the body, too often that theology overlooks the body's specificity or particularity or individuation in gender, race, culture, and society. Indeed, much of our theological language remains disturbingly innocent of the alienation, abuse, and disdain of certain bodies, even within the Church. On historical, cultural, and social fronts, the injurious impact of misogyny, racism, anti-Semitism, homophobia, and transphobia quite literally has robbed too many *bodypersons* of life and freedom, flourishing and joy. Ignoring particularity in the name of objectivity actually elicits uniformity that passes as false universality and privileges dominant groups.

The physical body of Jesus, our physical bodies, *all* physical human bodies are *marked*—rendering each of us individual and particular, different and distinct, vivid and personal in history through gender and race, sex and sexuality, culture and tradition. These marks may delight or unnerve, impose limitation or offer inclusion. Yet, history and human experience teach us about the ambiguities of those *bodymarks*, for they often elude physical, biological, and societal categories; destabilize gender identities whether socially conditioned or putatively "given"; unsettle communal and personal relationships; even warp decision and action. History and human experience also instruct us on how brutally and easily the value and significance of the body and that of *bodypersons* may be manipulated and violated. Indeed, such manipulation and violation defy the Christian notion that the body constitutes a site of divine revelation and is a "basic human sacrament."[1] For, it is in and through our very bodies that we *bodypersons* perceive, take, and carry out decisions that express our essential freedom concretely through engagement and communion with other *bodypersons*.

The cultural anthropologist Mary Douglas calls our attention to the body's symbolic function in human culture. She focuses on the body as a code or image for social reality, distinguishing and relating the physical and social bodies: "The social body constrains the way the physical body is perceived."[2] In other words, our interaction and engagement with others is crucial to realizing our essential freedom, but, that realization, in large measure, depends upon cultural perceptions and societally conditioned responses to our bodies. So, the social body's assignment of positive or negative meanings to race, gender, culture, sex, or sexuality may influence, even determine, the trajectories of the lived lives of bodypersons who differ from the arbitrary norm. "The body is in the social world," remarks French social theorist Pierre Bourdieu, "but the social world is in the body."[3] Thus, a social world shaped arbitrarily and exclusively in the image and likeness of any particular race, gender, sex, sexuality, or culture might assign power and privilege only to those in their particular group; at the same time, indifference or repressive action paves the way for that particular group to carry out subtle or grotesque cruelties upon those bodypersons who are different.

For theological anthropology, given the "fact of [Christian] faith that when God desires to manifest"[4] the divine presence, God does so in human flesh, the body can never be simply one element among others. Still, theological anthropology that takes the body and body marks seriously risks turning what can be seen (e.g., race and sex), culturally conditioned (e.g., gender), represented (e.g., sex/sexuality), expressed (e.g., culture), and regulated (e.g., social order) into absolutes. Furthermore, such theological attention to specific and particular characteristics also risks "fragmenting"[5] the human person. What makes this risk-taking imperative is the vulnerability of marginalized and oppressed bodypersons in our global context: consider the global recurrences of mass murders and genocides; the stubborn persistence of anti-Semitism, Islamophobia, anti-Black racism, sexism, and xenophobic reactions to so-called illegal migrant bodypersons; the malicious disrespect of bodypersons who are assaulted, abused, and raped; the vicious disregard of bodypersons who are tortured, maimed, starved, and slaughtered in war; and the global economy's cruel cannibalization of bodypersons for their labor and creativity, their sexuality and generativity. What makes this risk-taking obligatory is the marginalized Jewish body of Jesus of Nazareth, whose body was broken and resurrected for us *all*.

Through his life, death, and resurrection, Jesus shows us what it means to be a bodyperson. His compassionate solidaristic love and dynamic ministry releases the power of God's animating image and likeness in our red, brown, yellow, white, Black bodies—our LGBTQI and heterosexual bodies, our disease-infected bodies, our prostituted bodies, our yearning bodies, our debilitated bodies, our infirm bodies, our young and aging bodies, our enervated and joyous bodies. To stand silent before war and murder, incarceration and torture, rape and queer/trans-bashing, pain and disease, abuse of power and position renders us complicit in sacrilegious offense against the very body of God.

The body of the Jewish Jesus, the Christ of God, is the only body capable of taking us *all* in as we are with all our different body marks. His taking us in (*in-corporating* us) does not remove our individuality and distinctiveness, does not erase our body marks. Jesus draws us into him, calls us to discipleship in which we stand and act in solidarity with one another. Humble engagement in his ministry revalues our identities and differences, even as it preserves the integrity and significance of our body marks. At the same time, our particular body marks are reoriented and reappropriated under his sign, the sign of the cross. Thus, in solidarity, in love of others, in love of the Holy Other, we are re-made and re-marked as his body—the body of Christ. Thus, in fidelity to the God of Jesus, who is the God of life and love, theological anthropology can never cease speaking of bodies.

REFLECTION QUESTIONS

1. How do those around you mark or categorize your *bodyperson* (the totality of your embodiment)? How have these labels limited or empowered you?
2. What does "perfection in Jesus" mean if our physical human "imperfections," wounds, or illnesses remain?
3. Have you ever felt that your body was not "good enough" for Christ to be incarnate in? Can you name the teachings or experiences that support your feeling?
4. How do you acknowledge and celebrate that God chose to manifest God's self in the historical Jewish male body of Jesus of Nazareth?

SUGGESTED READING

Byron, Gay L., and Vanessa Lovelace, eds. *Womanist Interpretations of the Bible: Expanding the Discourse*. Atlanta: SBL Press, 2016.

Copeland, M. Shawn. *Enfleshing Freedom: Body, Race, and Being*. 2nd ed. Minneapolis: Fortress Press, 2023.

Diaz, Miguel H. *On Being Human: U.S. Hispanic and Rahnerian Perspectives*. Maryknoll, NY: Orbis Books, 2001.

Douglas, Kelly Brown. *Stand Your Ground: Black Bodies and the Justice of God*. Maryknoll, NY: Orbis Books, 2015.

Ellison, Marvin Mahan, and Kelly Brown Douglas, ed. *Sexuality and the Sacred: Sources for Theological Reflection*. 2nd ed. Louisville, KY: Westminster John Knox Press, 2010.

Farley, Margaret A. *Just Love: A Framework for Christian Sexual Ethics*. London: Continuum Books, 2008.

Farley, Wendy. *Gathering Those Driven Away: A Theology of Incarnation*. Louisville, KY: Westminster Press, 2011.

Himes, Kenneth R., and Conor M. Kelly. *Poverty: Responding Like Jesus*. Brewster, MA: Paraclete Press, 2018.

Isasi-Diaz, Ada Maria. *La Lucha Continues: Mujerista Theology*. Maryknoll, NY: Orbis Books, 1996.

Pineda-Madrid, Nancy. *Suffering and Salvation in Cuidad Juárez*. Minneapolis: Fortress Press, 2011.

Thurman, Howard. *Jesus and the Disinherited*. 1949; repr., Boston: Beacon Press, 1996.

Notes

1. Michael Scanlon, "Postmodernism and Theology," *The Ecumenist* 37, no. 2 (Spring 2000): 18.

2. Mary Douglas, *Natural Symbols: Explorations in Cosmology*, 2nd ed. (New York: Routledge, 1996), 73.

3. Pierre Bourdieu, *Pascalian Meditations* (Stanford: Stanford University Press, 2000), 152.

4. Karl Rahner, "The Body in the Order of Salvation," *Theological Investigations*, vol. XVII (New York: Crossroad, 1981), 74.

5. Carlo Maria Martini, *On the Body: A Contemporary Theology of the Human Person* (New York: Crossroad Publishing, 2001), 3.

6

BEAUTY AND THE HUMAN

An Encounter with Sor Juana Inés de la Cruz

Michelle Gonzalez Maldonado

A retrospective look at the short life of Sor Juana Inés de la Cruz is emblematic of ongoing challenges the Church faces as a result of a theological anthropology that continues to categorize women as ontologically inferior to men. Sor Juana lived in the second half of the seventeenth century in colonial Mexico, aka New Spain, and is considered one of the most influential authors in the Spanish language. She was an avid reader, primarily self-taught, and by her mid-teens was recognized as the most erudite woman in Mexico. Although she spent part of her life as a lady in waiting at the viceregal court under the tutelage of María Luisa Manrique de Lara y Gonzaga, Marquesa de Laguna, she was more enamored by the love of learning than of men and declined several marriage proposals, opting instead to take the veil and join the order of St. Jerome at the age of nineteen. Her time in the convent was focused primarily on intellectual study and scholarship of philosophy and the natural sciences; she was also a poet and playwright. Her writings incorporate an eclectic mixture of colonial Mexican philosophy and continental theology, including Thomism, Neoplatonism, and hermeticism. A child of the Americas, Sor Juana also incorporates Indigenous and African sources and voices throughout her corpus. One of her most significant contributions to Christian theology is her defense of Indigenous peoples and her understanding of Indigenous religions as a prefiguration of Christianity.

As she gained notoriety for her writings and commissioned works, she satirically criticized male clerics and intellectuals for their hypocrisy and misogyny in her famous poem, *Hombres necios*[1] (see link below). Within the span of thirty-three years her writings and creativity made her a force to be reckoned with, and her close relationship with Spanish nobility in Mexico benefited Sor Juana greatly. The Marquesa's noble status allowed her to provide gifts to advance Sor Juana's studies and simultaneously shielded her from the mounting jealousy and suspicions that surrounded Sor Juana within and beyond the convent walls. Eventually, however, her fame drew the negative attention of the Catholic hierarchy, who charged that no woman, let alone a nun, should be recognized for her brilliant writings, and her confessor publicly maligned her. Shortly thereafter, by an irrevocable political act, the Marques and Marquesa were called back to Spain, and Sor Juana was left without a guardian or a defense. Shortly after their departure, Sor Juana was forced to surrender all of her books and her instruments of scientific inquiry and submit to a life of humility and obedience. Fulfilling her vows, she took an additional vow of silence and renounced writing in what would become the final years of her life. When assigned to the infirmary during the plague, Sor Juana obliged and died caring for her sisters.

Sor Juana's "transgressions" were due to her intellectual prowess at a time when women were excluded from private or public engagement in theology, philosophy, or any rational science. One of Sor Juana's last writings is *La Respuesta a Sor Filotea* (*The Response*), her autobiographical justification for women's intelligence and their right to education and study. She makes an extended argument not only for her own God-given love of learning, but also for the recognition of the full humanity of women and the importance of their education. To build her case, she uses an exegesis of Pauline texts traditionally used to silence women; her own life story of an innate desire to learn; philosophical arguments based on the interrelated nature of all knowledge culminating in theology; historical arguments cataloging a list of women leaders and thinkers from a variety of sources, eras, and contexts; and an array of rhetorical arts.

In one section of *The Response*, Sor Juana tells of a time when the Inquisition forbade her from reading for three months. While preventing her from studying texts, the prohibition was not capable of ensnaring her mind. Instead of studying books, she observed the world around her and studied daily life. Her study of the architecture of the dormitories led to lessons on geometry. The pleasure of watching two girls playing with tops turned the exercise into a scientific experiment with flour, along with other experiments in the kitchen with eggs, that led to a wealth of knowledge. On these culinary experiments she writes, "What can women know if not philosophies of the kitchen?" Sor Juana sarcastically challenges the caricature that the activities of life are gender-coded, as women are somehow thoughtless and lacking in intellectual valor. This comment is closely followed by perhaps one of the most delightful statements in her corpus, "Had Aristotle cooked, he would have written a great deal more."

What is the significance of the anecdotes Sor Juana shares about her daily life? In equating the knowledge acquired in women's private sphere to that of the great philosophers and theologians she read extensively, Sor Juana constitutes woman's private arena as a space for rational reflection. While not offering a systematic critique of women's place in society, Sor Juana changes the very significance and meaning of that space and place. Intuitively, she transforms the very nature of the theological task through the aesthetic form of her theology. This also leads to a new understanding of the human, one that recognizes the full humanity of women.

This anthropology is also found in Sor Juana's villancicos devoted to Saint Catherine of Alexandria. A villancico is a poem with short lines that was sung, in Sor Juana's time, on religious holidays. One of the villancicos is a defense of the intellectual rights of women and the spiritual equality of men and women. Sor Juana states in her poem that biological sex has no role in one's intellect and claims that God intended women to serve the Church through their intelligence. This poem is an example of Sor Juana's public denouncement of the role society and the Church have assigned her. Like St. Catherine, Sor Juana sees herself as a woman whose intellect is a gift of God, yet whose biological sex has turned into a curse within her gendered societal constraints.

The literary form of the majority of Sor Juana's corpus poses a methodological challenge to contemporary theology by revealing the organic relationship between beauty and justice within historical and contemporary theology. Through her introduction of the aesthetic within the theological task, Sor Juana makes the symbolic a privileged form of theology, stating that the aesthetic is *the most appropriate form* of theological expression. An emphasis on the aesthetic is grounded in the belief that within the realm of symbol, imagination, emotion, and art one finds a privileged expression of the encounter with the divine and its articulation. Accompanying the aesthetic form of her theology is an interdisciplinary understanding of theology that saturates Sor Juana's corpus. Theology is not merely limited to what contemporary scholars deem today "theological" texts. Instead, literature, poetry, and drama become central forms of theological expression. For example, at the center of theological aesthetics is the importance of the interrelationship between aesthetics and ethics. The good, beauty, and the true must remain organically united, existing in their interrelationship. Beauty is not a distraction from justice, but instead the motivation behind and a means of expressing justice as right relation. Theological aesthetics redefines how one can speak authentically about the religious dimension of humanity.

How can Sor Juana's theological aesthetics help us to navigate a renewed theological understanding of our humanity? Today we live in a postpandemic world, and the acute fragility of our humanity and our vulnerabilities lead to a sense of brokenness because of the persistence of fear, oppression, and the weaponizing of bodies. We hear immigrants being labeled as animals, and women and children being trafficked and sexually commodified or disappeared, denying the integrity of their humanity. We are confronted with an increasing mental health crisis among young people, accompanied by a growing sense of hopelessness and inability to resolve conflicts and disagreements in a respectful manner. Where is beauty?

Sor Juana would tell us that beauty is in our encounter with the sacred and with each other. She would remind us to ask the question, "What moves the human heart?" as posed by my former mentor, the late Alejandro García-Rivera. Sor Juana would also remind us that in that direct encounter with beauty, or the sacred, which often happens in our everyday life, the image of God is revealed within each of us. Creation reveals a supernatural orientation toward the sacred wherein all of humanity shares in this common human nature. We are created to be in relationship with God through the good, the beautiful, and the true. The image of God within us is not stagnant; it evolves as dynamic and alive. Our growth in the image of God is part of our self-discovery of who we are as creatures of the divine. This leads to a dramatic anthropology where the human is in a continual evolutionary process of becoming. The notion of creation in the image of God is highly abstract. To be meaningful, theological reflections on that image must always be grounded in concrete everyday lives with an awareness of how power, prejudice, and privilege can distort this dynamic beauty. If the pinnacle of God's self-revelation within and among the ordinariness of creation is the sacred act of the incarnation of beauty, as Sor Juana's works propose, how is humanity to respond to this divine gesture?

REFLECTION QUESTIONS

1. As modeled in the life of Sor Juana Inés de la Cruz, who exemplified her call to explore truth,

and discover beauty as revelatory of the divine, when or how has beauty been a vehicle of the sacred, of truth, or of justice in your life?
2. What would it mean to privilege the aesthetic as the most authentic expression of the sacred and as the most authentic description of who we are as human beings?
3. How would serious consideration of everyday life as a source of theology broaden our understandings of theological sources and authority?

SUGGESTED READING

Gonzalez, Michelle A. *Sor Juana: Beauty and Justice in the Americas*. Maryknoll, NY: Orbis Books, 2003.

Hinsdale, Mary Ann, and Stephen Okey. *T&T Clark Handbook of Theological Anthropology*. New York: T&T Clark, 2021.

Saracino, Michelle. *Christian Anthropology: An Introduction to the Human Person*. Mahwah, NJ: Paulist Press, 2015.

Yugar, Theresa A. *Sor Juana Inés de la Cruz: Feminist Reconstruction of Biography and Text*. Eugene, OR: Wipf and Stock, 2014.

Notes

1. "Hombres necios que acusáis," AP Spanish Literature, English translation, http://www.apspanishliterature.com/2011/10/hombres-necios-que-acusais.html.

7

WE ARE HISPANIC/ LATINÉ CATHOLICS, *SOMOS SERES HUMANOS*[1]

Hosffman Ospino

We are often unaware of how strongly race and ethnicity mold our notion of the meaning of "being human." For example, few expressions trigger more passionate responses or capture the imagination of theologians, sociologists, politicians, artists, and many others as the "Browning of America." At the heart of that process is the Hispanicization of our nation.[2] There are about 64 million Hispanics in the United States, of whom nearly 45 percent self-identify as Catholic. Yet, we live in a society in which millions ignore the basic fact that before the Mayflower dropped anchor, Hispanics had already settled in this land. American historical accounts scantily recognize the histories of conquest and colonization that shaped the memory of Hispanic cultures. How does the complex history of Hispanic/Latinos in the United States challenge the Catholic Church to ask critical questions of the sociopolitical institutions that often delegitimize the inherent dignity of marginalized Hispanic communities within its borders? How would a renewed Christian anthropology require a revisioning of our human interconnectedness as members of the Body of Christ?

The history of Hispanics in the United States can be likened to a colorful tapestry woven by many hands for more than five centuries. It is a tapestry made of multiple narratives, linked intimately to the stories that give life to the many other groups that constitute the fabric of this society, making us one nation. For centuries, Hispanics have been forging something distinctive with the rest of our sisters and brothers with whom we share the American experience. No argument, political or religious, can erase the fact that, despite our differences, we all share in a common humanity which is not determined by the color of our skin, the language that we speak, or our gendered identities. We are, *Somos*. The "Browning of America" is a return to the vision of what we were meant to be from the beginning.

Our history, shaped by multiple origins and cultural roots, is complex. Our ability to name ourselves in multiple ways is often confronted with the use of the superimposed categories that aim to capture the essence of who we are or simply reduce us to someone's limited understanding of our experience. At the crossroads of multicultural communities, transnational economies, borderland politics, and forms of Christianity that blend the global with the local, Hispanic/Latiné populations in the United States define ourselves with fluidity given the particularities of our cultures. Such ways confront and defy the naïve, oppressive, and often violent impulses of those who erroneously feel compelled to tell us who we are.

The "Browning of America" brings to the fore critical anthropological questions resulting from the sociopolitical othering of nonwhite communities. The persistent endurance of Hispanic/Latiné communities in the United States, often living under dehumanizing conditions, alerts us to the inadequacy of predominant cultural and religious definitions of humanity and the qualities that such definitions presuppose. American society, including many of our own churches, manages to be silent and indifferent before the 65 percent increase in hate crimes targeting "Brown" populations since 2018 and the 85 percent increase in targeted violence against Hispanics since 2019.[3] Violence motivated by hate in a nation where the majority of its population self-identifies as Christian is evidence that our churches either are failing to form people's consciences authentically with the principles of the gospel, or their message of life and hope has been shamelessly corrupted by ideology that condones racism and death. Nonetheless, our response to this violence as Hispanics remains a persistent holding fast onto our faith, memories, traditions, and family, despite the struggles for recognition of our personhood and the fundamental affirmation of our human dignity. Retrieving and centering the many narratives of Hispanic/Latiné communities, and how we have resisted evil throughout history, offers everyone in this society an opportunity to reclaim important elements of our shared value and dignity as one human family.

Regardless of how, when, and why people arrived, or were born in this country, the Hispanic/Latiné presence is a constant reminder that we are a nation shaped by multiple diasporas. Contemplating the particularity of our diverse experiences makes us more aware of the great mystery of being human and more ethically responsible vis-à-vis the demands that this mystery imposes upon us as members of a broader society.

WE ARE HISPANIC/ LATINÉ CATHOLICS...

Because most Hispanics in the United States are heirs of the Catholic faith through affiliation or cultural association, it is important to acknowledge the various ways Catholic Christianity has influenced our understanding of what it means to be human. Our resilience amid suffering, our sense of community, our love for the family, our knowing ourselves as belonging to the land and the larger created order upon which we depend, and many expressions of solidarity with those most vulnerable, among others, are gifts we bring into this society. *Somos seres humanos y somos hermanos y hermanas*—we are human beings; we are brothers and sisters.

Theologians and pastoral leaders recognize the immense power of popular Catholicism as a vehicle to celebrate, interpret, and pass on the faith from one generation to the next. Liturgical life holds a special place in the religious imagination of Hispanic Catholics. The rise of apostolic movements (e.g., the Catholic Charismatic Renewal, Cursillo) promises a new wave of spiritual revitalization. All these experiences point to a sense of *mística* (mystical) that offers a lens through which Hispanic Catholics see and understand ourselves as human beings in the world—a place where God comes to our encounter and affirms our inherent dignity *en lo cotidiano* (the everyday).

Many of us are here because the horrors of terrorism and large-scale violence, sociopolitical oppression, repression, violence, and the disappearance of persons in Latin America and the Caribbean have driven millions to leave their lands and seek new opportunities in North America. Anti-immigrant sentiments, racism, classism, and a misguided Christian nationalist alliance between faith and politics threaten the lives and well-being of Hispanics and other minoritized communities who have called the United States home for centuries, as well as asylum seekers, and others in diaspora. Remaining silent and indifferent is not an option if we are to prophetically defend human dignity—particularly in the name of Christ.

To respond to these challenges, Hispanic Catholics must continue to draw from the best of our Roman Catholic tradition and the richness of our cultural and historical experiences by embracing the *preferential option for the poor* in new and profoundly transformative ways. In addition, we must ask poignantly, What is the Catholic Church doing to affirm the human dignity of Hispanics, especially the poorest among the poor? How might Catholic communities provide hope for persons seeking opportunity? What more can the Church do to promote quality education—Catholic and public—that effectively moves our young out of cycles of poverty and invisibility? Will Catholic citizens vote to support policies that address the disproportionate rates of imprisonment, the proliferation of immigrant detention centers, the threat of massive deportations, and the separation of children from immigrants and asylum seekers at the border?

Because the people most affected by these realities are young Hispanics, these questions challenge us all to make a *preferential option for our Hispanic youth*, who constitute the majority of the U.S. Catholic population younger than thirty. Making a *preferential option for Hispanic families*, in their many forms and expressions, is investing in the future of our society and our faith communities. Hispanic families and communities experience much struggle, particularly from an idealized view of family life that privileges patriarchy and machismo. Being Hispanic Catholics in the United States offers us the opportunity to reimagine family life and accompaniment in ways that better affirm the dignity of those most vulnerable, especially Hispanic women and children.

We are Hispanic, Latino/a, Latiné, Latinx, *indígenas*, Hispanic-American, *estadounidenses*. Our presence, stories and voices together, constitute our gift, and our greatest challenge to church and society in the United States. Together we ponder what it means to be human in our day, and question whether all is not lost when the recognition of the inherent dignity of self is not reflected in the lives of "the other."

REFLECTION QUESTIONS

1. "The 'Browning of America' is a return to the vision of what we were meant to be from the beginning." Do you agree with this affirmation? Yes/No/Why?
2. What do you find compelling about the Hispanic Catholic experience, and—whether you are Hispanic or not—how does it challenge you to live your Catholicism in new ways?
3. What are you doing—or what can you do—as a Catholic to speak prophetically against the realities that deny or diminish the human dignity of Hispanic people in our society?

SUGGESTED READING

De la Torre, Miguel. *Trails of Hope and Terror: Testimonies on Immigration*. Maryknoll, NY: Orbis, 2009.

Elizondo, Virgilio. *The Future Is Mestizo: Life Where Cultures Meet*. Rev. ed. Boulder, CO: University Press of Colorado, 2000.

Espín, Orlando. *Grace and Humanness: Theological Reflections Because of Culture*. Maryknoll, NY: Orbis, 2013.

Goizueta, Roberto. Caminemos Con Jesus*: Toward a Hispanic/Latino Theology of Accompaniment*. Maryknoll, NY: Orbis Books, 1995.

González, Juan. *Harvest of Empire: A History of Latinos in America*. Rev. ed. New York: Penguin Books, 2011.

Imperatori-Lee, Natalia. Cuéntame*: Narrative in the Ecclesial Present*. Maryknoll, NY: Orbis, 2018.

Pineda-Madrid, Nancy. *Theologizing in an Insurgent Key: Violence, Women, Salvation*. New York: Paulist Press, 2022.

Romero, Robert Chao. *Brown Church: Five Centuries of Latina/o Social Justice, Theology, and Identity*. Downers Grove, IL: InterVarsity Press, 2020.

United States Conference of Catholic Bishops. *Strangers No Longer: Together on the Journey of Hope. A Pastoral Letter Concerning Migration from the Catholic Bishops of Mexico and the United States*. Washington, DC: USCCB, 2003.

Notes

1. This chapter is an updated adaptation of a longer article I published previously. See Hosffman Ospino, "Called and Sent to Encuentro: A Pastoral Theological Vision for the Fifth Encuentro Process," *Origins* 44, no. 43 (April 2015): 705–9.

2. Felipe Fernández-Armesto, *Our America: A Hispanic His-*

tory of the United States (New York: W.W. Norton & Company, 2014).

3. Marlene Lenthang, "El Paso Walmart Shooter Who Targeted Hispanics Agrees to Pay Families More Than $5 Million," NBC News, September 25, 2023, https://www.nbcnews.com/news/us-news/texas-shooter-targeted-hispanics-2019-walmart-rampage-agrees-pay-5-mil-rcna117235.

8

A SKETCH OF A LIBERATIVE NATURAL LAW ANTHROPOLOGY

Craig A. Ford Jr.

There are many idioms through which one might articulate the contours of a theological anthropology. In choosing a natural law idiom, I am taking a challenging road, since over the course of the last millennium the natural law has been used, and continues to be used, in service of a number of dehumanizing and immoral agendas. These agendas emerge, for example, when language about "nature" is used for misogynistic or sexist ends, as witnessed during the centuries of European colonization. In this period, "nature" and arguments based in the natural law were used to justify the expropriation of lands from, as well as the enslavement of, native populations. Today, natural law arguments feature strongly in denunciations of homosexuality and transgender identity, as well as in the subjugation of women. But a different articulation of a natural law anthropology—a genuinely *liberative* articulation of a natural law anthropology—is possible. Such a project, founded on Thomas Aquinas's own method for discerning human flourishing, bases itself on the observation that we are all by nature designed for, and capable of, loving God. Crucially, for us human beings this natural love for God unfolds through our pursuit of the truth imprinted upon us like a divine light. This imprint—what Thomas calls that natural law—leads us to honor all that we have learned and continue to learn about human nature scientifically and philosophically. These affirmations lead us to a number of convictions, among which are that the natural law can no longer be used to buttress the evil forces of white supremacy, misogyny, heterosexism, as well as the other forms of violence and oppression that marginalize people.

The sins committed in the name of the natural law notwithstanding, I do think that it is worth reclaiming in anthropological projects, because the theory itself can be regarded as illuminating what it means for human beings to flourish. I hold these convictions on both intellectual and moral grounds. The natural law is not a single *theory* but a *tradition* of ethical reasoning. As such, some schools of natural law thinking—in particular the revisionist strands advocated by thinkers like Jean Porter, Lisa Cahill, Cristina Traina, Margaret Farley, Stephen Pope, and Todd Salzman and Michael Lawler—are more promising than others and could be further developed to address diverse contexts. On the other hand, the central *moral* motivation for reclaiming the natural law lay in the duty to make reparation for the damage committed in its name. Weaponized natural law theories have inflicted suffering and death on millions of people. Reclaiming the natural law for liberative ends means removing its oppressive and death-dealing sting for good. This project takes on special urgency for members of the LGBTQ+ community, whose lives and loves are denounced by many Christians in the name of the natural law without contemporary considerations from the natural and social sciences and their implications for the natural law itself.

A sketch of such a liberative natural law anthropology would begin with a fundamental conviction shared across all natural law strands: that the human being, like the rest of creation, goes forth from the heart of God with the goal of returning to that very heart. This model of creation's origin and destiny, known as *exitus-reditus* (exit-return), is important to natural law thinking, because it provides the organizing structure for the *Summa Theologiae* (*ST*) of Thomas Aquinas, the famous thirteenth-century Dominican and saint.[1] Thomas also highlights what makes the human being distinct within earthly creation: that we, by nature, are designed to love, and are capable of loving, God. This is what it means to be made *imago Dei*, or in the image of God (*ST* I 93.4).

But how do we accomplish this love of God? How do we live into our nature? Thomas says that we are creatures of insatiable curiosity: we seek to love God by learning as much as we possibly can about this God. Unlike angels—heavenly creatures who are capable of loving God (*ST* I 60)—we human beings come to greater love of God through our *embodied* interaction with the world that God has created. In other words, for us, growing in love of God comes by way of sense (because we have bodies) and by way of science (because we want to know the truth).

Crucially, this dual aspect of human knowledge—sense and science—is buoyed by God's grace. This is an important point. For Thomas, God remains the origin of our knowing, even when we are ignorant of something, or when our reasoning fails. To illustrate this, Thomas uses the image of God as light that illuminates our minds. Sealing his argument is a quote from Psalms:

> "Many say: Who showeth us good things?" which question the Psalmist answers, "The light of Thy countenance, O Lord, is signed upon us," as though he were to say: By the seal of the Divine light in us, all things are made known to us. (*ST* I 84.5, quoting Ps 4:6–7)

This quote from Psalms also emerges in the passage where Thomas considers the natural law:

> Hence the Psalmist after saying (Psalm 4:6): "Offer up the sacrifice of justice," as though someone asked what the works of justice are, adds: "Many say, Who showeth us good things?" in answer to which question he says: "The light of Thy countenance, O Lord, is signed upon us": thus implying that the light of natural reason, whereby we discern what is good and what is evil, which is the function of the natural law, is nothing else than an imprint on us of the Divine light. It is therefore evident that the natural law is nothing else than the rational creature's participation of the eternal law. (*ST* I-II 91.2)

For our purposes, the significance of these two passages is this: God rests as the principle not only of our knowledge of things in the natural world, but also of our knowledge of moral truth. This means that moral knowledge must also be something that we learn, by sense and by science, over time, through the expansion of our understanding of what is natural.

Thomas also indicates that we come to know the natural law *by inclination*: we are drawn to certain goods simply in virtue of our existence (*ST* I–II 94.2). But this is not to say that discerning the natural law is obvious. In fact, discerning the requirements of the natural law in a particular situation can be quite difficult (*ST* I–II 94.4). This is the reason why we need the virtues, which help us become morally excellent beings (*ST* I–II 56.1). From here, various natural law accounts of the sorts of actions and dispositions that best realize the life of virtue diverge. Thomas himself goes down a number of roads alongside which a liberative natural law cannot follow. He embraces misogynistic beliefs about women as "defective and misbegotten" (*ST* I 92.1, ad. 1). He also regards all same-sex sexual behavior as vicious and lustful (*ST* II–II 154.11). Given what we know about women and about homosexuality, these conclusions are no longer tenable.

However, one can embrace Thomas's natural law method while moving beyond his thirteenth-century conclusions. In fact, a natural law anthropology actually *demands* that one move beyond thirteenth-century conclusions, given the understanding that God intends us to be creatures who learn, by sense and by science, the nature of the world that God created. For us, this means paying close attention to what we are learning about the complexity and beauty of the natural world.

As I've pointed out elsewhere, the Church has had to learn difficult lessons regarding magisterial fallibility when it erroneously condemned Galileo as a heretic for teaching—and as we know in hindsight now rightly teaching—that the earth revolves around the sun. This story serves as a cautionary tale for us today on the topics of sexuality and gender identity: the Church must not, as it did in the seventeenth century, close itself off to emerging scientific insight. To do this, the Church must embrace a posture of humility in order to learn the truths that both the natural and social sciences are offering regarding sexual orientation and gender identity. The Church must acknowledge more of the complex particularities of human embodiment than it has acknowledged in its official teaching. Thomas used the best science of his day; the Church should not deprive itself of the best and most accurate knowledge at its disposal.

There are two reasons why so depriving ourselves of this emerging knowledge would be disastrous. One reason, as I mentioned at the beginning, is that continuing to misuse the natural law as a weapon of oppression will prove disastrous for those on the underside of history. A second reason, if we take Thomas seriously, is that such misuse of the natural law actually results in the willful occlusion of the divine light meant to guide us not only into truth about the world, but also toward a deeper understanding of the meaning of being human. Knowing who, and whose, we are, returns us into the heart of God. We literally cannot be fully human, as God desires, without that light.

REFLECTION QUESTIONS

1. Ford writes that natural law theories have been used in ways that promote evils like racism, homophobia, transphobia, and misogyny. Do you agree with this? Do you likewise believe that it is possible to use natural law theology in a liberative mode?

2. The seventeenth-century Galileo affair constituted an episode in the Church's past where it failed to be open to emerging scientific insight. Do you believe that the Church can learn from this past when engaging contemporary topics related to sexuality and gender identity?
3. Following Thomas Aquinas, Ford understands the natural law as an imprint upon us of the divine light that guides us toward human flourishing. In what ways is the divine light imprinted upon you guiding you toward flourishing?

SUGGESTED READINGS

Farley, Margaret. *Just Love: A Framework for Christian Sexual Ethics*. New York: Continuum, 2008.

Ford, Craig A., Jr. "Born That Way? The Challenge of Trans/Gender Identity for Catholic Theology." In *Sex, Love and Families: Catholic Perspectives*, edited by Julie Hanlon Rubio and Jason King, 91–101. Collegeville, MN: Liturgical Press, 2020.

———. "Our New Galileo Affair." *Horizons* 50, no 2 (December 2023): 255–92.

Salzman, Todd, and Michael Lawler. *The Sexual Person: Toward a Renewed Catholic Anthropology*. Washington, DC: Georgetown University Press, 2008.

Notes

1. Thomas Aquinas, *Summa Theologiae*. Translated by Fathers of the English Dominican Province. 5 vols. New York: Benzinger Bros, 1948.

9

COMPLEMENTARITY AND HUMAN DIGNITY

Correction of Confused Catholic Doctrine

Todd A. Salzman and Michael G. Lawler

Over the last sixty years, the Vatican as well as Catholic theologians have been preoccupied with the questions, What makes a sexual union worthy of human beings, as embodied persons created in the image of God? What makes sex both holy and human? Is sexuality an essential dimension of being human? The Vatican has argued that a holy sexual union must join partners whose genitals are complementary and who could, in theory, conceive and bring a child into the world as a result of that union. We call this inadequate vision of the person *genital complementarity*. Instead, we believe *holistic complementarity* honors the infinite variety of spiritual, emotional, and intellectual qualities that God instills in us, which have little to do with our genitals. We make a case for this more robust, holistic vision, which, despite its respect for LGBTQ+ persons, the new document *Dignitas Infinita* does not support.

In his 1981 apostolic exhortation *Familiaris Consortio*, Pope John Paul II introduced the term *complementarity* into official Catholic teaching, and official Church documents have continued to use the term to justify the Church's restriction of moral sexual activity to gender-complementary sexual acts open to transmission of life within a heterosexual marriage. For John Paul, complementarity means that certain realities belong together and produce a whole that neither can produce alone. While every person is complete individually, as a member of a couple, each person needs to be completed by relation to the other. Sexual complementarity, John Paul argues, completes a couple in marriage by bringing the masculine and feminine biological elements together in a unified whole, in the sexual acts that are moral in marriage.

According to the *Catechism* (n. 2357) biological and personal dimensions of complementarity are intrinsically linked and inseparable, yet Church documents continue to prioritize biological complementarity, which applies both to functioning male and female genitalia and to biologically reproductive-type sexual acts that are open to the transmission of life. This means that, according to the *Catechism*, the sine qua non for moral sexual acts is grounded in biology, genitalia, and reproductive-type sexual acts. Only if biological complementarity is present can we even discuss the unitive, personal complementarity between any two people that the Catholic Church now teaches is an end of marriage equal to procreation. Personal complementarity includes communion, affective, and parental complementarities. Communion complementarity is the two-in-oneness created by every just and loving relationship. Affective complementarity is the integrated loving, personal, social, and spiritual elements of human persons grounded in relationship. Parental complementarity is the complementarity of parents who fulfill the second dimension of procreation, namely, the education of children, who need both masculine and feminine models. The Congregation for the Doctrine of the Faith (CDF) insists that same-sex couples and parents do not meet any of the requirements for these complementarities and teaches, for instance, contrary to abundant scientific evidence, same-sex parents "do violence" to children in their care.

In an address to the CDF, Pope Francis introduces a more nuanced notion of complementarity, acknowledging an evolving understanding of the concept and, from a progressive perspective, laying the foundation for both anthropological and doctrinal developments. Francis's first nuance is an important emphasis on complementarity as a dynamic and evolving idea rather than a "simplistic idea that all the roles and relations of both sexes are confined to a single and static model." His second nuance is that family as an "anthropological fact" cannot be qualified by "ideological concepts which are compelling at only one moment in history, and then decline." There are now single-parent families, stepparent families, adoptive-parent families, foster-parent families, polygamous- and monogamous-parent families, and same-sex parent families. In each of these cases "family is family," and we must engage the reality we find, not what we would like to find. We must also evaluate the nature of the relationship between parents and their children based on sound scientific evidence, not on unjustified speculative prejudgments.[1]

We welcome Francis's spirit of openness and his support of same-sex civil unions. The approval of Catholic blessings for people in same-sex relationships in *Fiducia Supplicans* signals a development in Church thinking, even though more anthropological and doctrinal development must occur to overcome confusion over the Church's pastoral openness toward, versus its doctrinal rejection of, LGBTQ+ persons. Specifically, the Church's insistence that personal complementarity is based in, and dependent upon, genital, heterosexual difference is confused. Its further insistence that other kinds of sexual relationships and all nonreproductive sexual acts always frustrate personal complementarity and human dignity is equally confused. In essence, the Church's teaching regarding moral sexual activity reduces human beings to their genitals.

However, we agree that holy sexual unions do involve complementarity of a different kind. We propose a concept that we name holistic complementarity. Holistic complementarity ontologically prioritizes the relational over the biological in human relationship and, in light of a person's sexual orientation, emphasizes personal, affective, and spiritual union in sexual relationships. Heterogenital complementarity is needed for reproduction, but it is not needed for the complementary personal, affective, spiritual connection between two persons that the recent Catholic tradition acknowledges as an end of marriage or meaning of the sexual act equal to procreation. Same-sex couples can certainly exhibit this holistic complementarity. According to holistic complementarity, sexual acts can take any form that is just, honest, and loving and promotes human dignity. Scientific and experiential witness overwhelmingly support the fact that such acts promote and sustain healthy and nurturing relationships and parenting for both heterosexual and same-sex couples. Holistic complementarity includes orientation, personal, and neurobiological complementarity, and the integration and manifestation of all three in just, honest, loving, committed sexual acts that facilitate a person's ability to love God, neighbor, and self in more profound and holy ways.

In light of holistic complementarity, we advance the following with regard to Catholic sexual doctrines and ethical sexual acts. Sexual doctrines must be formulated, and moral sexual acts must be defined, in light of a revised theological anthropology grounded in holistic, not heterogenital, complementarity. A person's sexual orientation is a fundamental dimension of their human nature and dignity, and sexual doctrines that prescribe or proscribe specific sexual acts must be formulated and applied in light of the particular nature and orientation of the person. Sexual doctrines must seek to facilitate the integration of holistic complementarity. This integration does not allow for the absolute condemnation of particular sexual acts without due consideration of a person's sexual orientation and how persons in complementary relationships experience intimacy—which may or may not be expressed in and through genital (not necessarily heterogenital) complementarity. Whereas the Church's model posits absolute doctrines forbidding homosexual acts and nonreproductive sexual acts for heterosexual married couples, our holistic model cannot justify these absolutist doctrines.

Instead, we propose that holistic complementarity determine whether an act of sexual intimacy is moral or immoral. Holistic complementarity takes into account a person's sexual orientation alongside their innate human dignity, recently reaffirmed, confirmed, and lauded in the Vatican document *Dignitas Infinita* from the Dicastery for the Doctrine of the Faith (April 8, 2024). We pass over without comment the description of *human* dignity as infinite (a description contrary to the standard Catholic doctrine that only God is infinite) to what the document says about human dignity: "Every human person possesses an infinite dignity, inalienably grounded is his or her very being, which prevails in and beyond every circumstance, state, or situation the person may ever encounter." The Church, it continues, "resolutely reiterates and confirms the ontological dignity of the human person created in the image and likeness of God and redeemed in Jesus Christ" (n. 1). The dignity of the human person is not only an innately natural reality but by their very being as a human person, also an innately religious reality as created by God and redeemed by Jesus.

Dignitas Infinita concludes with a listing of "some specific and grave violations" (n. 33) of the human dignity it has so strongly asserted. No rational Christian would disagree with most of them. War, murder, genocide, poverty, subhuman living conditions, slavery, degrading working conditions, human trafficking, sexual abuse, violence against women, and abortion are all clearly grave violations against human dignity. Each and every one of these violations deserves commentary. We wish to comment only on the treatment of what is packed under the generalized and scientifically unsupported heading of "Gender Theory" (nn. 55–60). In this section, the dignity assigned to *every* human being is denied to transgender and gender-diverse persons, with unsubstantiated arguments.

Are we to assume, then, that some humans are not fully human? We see Jesus's parable of the Good Samaritan exemplified here. The priest and the Levite, representing the law and the prophets, pass by the man who has been robbed, stripped, and beaten, and they turn a blind eye to his need and humanity. Instead, it is the Samaritan, who is judged with disdain, who recognizes the man's need and is moved to act with compassion, takes him to safety, and pays for his care. Following Pope Francis's *Fratelli Tutti* (nn. 56–86), the institutional Catholic Church would be well served by an examination of conscience, and a renewed discernment of who is "the neighbor" to the countless people injured by exclusionary and oppressive doctrines that do not account for the inherent dignity of all God's people.

Dignitas Infinita (n. 55) and the *Catechism*'s teaching (n. 2358) that "every sign of unjust discrimination" against LGBTQ+ people "should be avoided" promotes so-called just discrimination against them and renders the Church's doctrinal teaching more representative of the attitude of the priest and Levite than the Samaritan. There is no place in holistic complementarity or the Church's profession of infinite human dignity for just discrimination against people based on their sexual orientation or just and loving relationships.

REFLECTION QUESTIONS

1. What is your own experience of intimate relations and their capacity to be procreative and unitive?
2. What type of complementarity is most often experienced within your human relationships?
3. What is your view on, and experience of, the relationship between your bodily sex—as male,

female, or intersex—and your gender expression—as masculine, feminine, or nonbinary?

4. How have your relationships formed your understanding of sexual human dignity? What are the implications of this understanding for Catholic sexual doctrines?

SUGGESTED READING

Farley, Margaret A. *Just Love: A Framework for Christian Sexual Ethics*. New York: Continuum, 2006.

Fullam, Lisa. "Sex in 3-D: A *Telos* for a Virtue Ethics of Sexuality." *Journal of the Society of Christian Ethics* 27, no. 2 (2007): 151–70.

Jung, Patricia Beattie, with Joseph Andrew Coray, eds. *Sexual Diversity and Catholicism: Toward the Development of Moral Theology*. Collegeville, MN: Liturgical Press, 2001. Available at https://muse.jhu.edu/pub/294/edited_volume/book/46576.

Lawler, Michael G., and Todd A. Salzman. "Pope Francis Brings Nuance to Notion of Complementarity." *National Catholic Reporter*, June 4, 2015. Available at http://ncronline.org/news/theology/pope-francis-brings-nuance-notion-complementarity.

———. "The Catholic Church Must Listen to Transgender and Intersex People: Male-Female Binary Leads to Discrimination and Bullying." *National Catholic Reporter*, December 1, 2020. Available at https://www.ncronline.org/news/opinion/catholic-church-must-listen-transgender-and-intersex-people.

———. "Sex, Gender, and Intersex: Anthropological, Medical, and Ethical Critiques and Proposals." *Theology and*

Sexuality 25, no. 3 (2019): 205–26. Available at https://www.tandfonline.com/doi/abs/10.1080/13558358.2020.1722563?scroll=top&needAccess=true&journalCode=yths20.

McCarthy, David Matzko. "The Relationship of Bodies: A Nuptial Hermeneutics of Same-Sex Unions." *Theology and Sexuality* 8 (1998): 96–112.

Salzman, Todd A. and Michael G. Lawler. *Pope Francis, Marriage, and Same-Sex Civil Unions: Foundations for the Organic Development of Catholic Sexual Doctrine*. Lanham, MD: Rowman & Littlefield, 2024.

———. *Sexual Ethics: A Theological Introduction*. Washington, DC: Georgetown University Press, 2012.

Notes

1. Pope Francis, "Address of His Holiness Pope Francis to Participants in the International Colloquium on the Complementarity between Man and Woman, Sponsored by the Congregation for the Doctrine of the Faith" (November 17, 2014), https://www.vatican.va/content/francesco/en/speeches/2014/november/documents/papa-francesco_20141117_congregazione-dottrina-fede.html.

CONTRIBUTORS

Tina Beattie is Professor Emerita of Catholic Studies at the University of Roehampton in London. She is the author of *God's Mother, Eve's Advocate* and *New Catholic Feminism: Theology and Theory*, among other books.

M. Shawn Copeland is Professor Emerita in the Department of Theology at Boston College. She is the author of *Enfleshing Freedom: Body, Race, and Being* and *Knowing Christ Crucified*, among other books.

Ilia Delio, OSF, holds the Josephine C. Connelly Endowed Chair in Theology at Villanova University and is founder of the Center for Christogenesis. She is the author of *The Emergent Christ* and *The Unbearable Wholeness of Being: God Evolution and the Power of Love*, among other books.

Craig A. Ford Jr. is assistant professor of theology and religious studies at St. Norbert College. He is the author of the forthcoming book *Works of Art: Sexuality, Gender, Race, and a New Theology of Embodiment*.

Daniel Horan is professor of philosophy, religious studies, and theology and Director of the Center for the Study of Spirituality at Saint Mary's College. He is the author of *Catholicity and Emerging Personhood: A Contemporary Theological Anthropology*, among others.

Elizabeth A. Johnson, CSJ, is Distinguished Professor Emerita of Theology at Fordham University. She is the author of *She Who Is: The Mystery of God in Feminist Theological Discourse* and *Come, Have Breakfast: Meditations on God and the Earth*, among others.

Michael G. Lawler is Professor Emeritus of Systematic Theology at Creighton University. He is the author of many books, many coauthored with Todd Salzman, including *Sexual Ethics: A Theological Introduction* and *Introduction to Catholic Theological Ethics: Foundations and Applications*.

Michelle Gonzalez Maldonado is professor of theology and religious studies at the University of Scranton. She is the author of *Created in God's Image: An Introduction to Feminist Theological Anthropology* and editor of *The Oxford Handbook of Caribbean Religions*, among others.

Elsie M. Miranda is Director of Culture and Community Engagement at The Association of Theological Schools. She is the coeditor of *Hispanic Ministry in the 21st Century: Urgent Matters*, and author of articles on theological and pastoral ethics.

Hosffman Ospino is Professor of Hispanic Ministry and Religious Education at Boston College Clough School of Theology and Ministry. He is the author of *Ministry with Young Hispanic Catholics: Towards a Recipe for Growth and Success*, among others.

Susan A. Ross is Professor Emerita of Theology at Loyola University Chicago. She is the author of *Anthropology: Seeking Light and Beauty* and *For the Beauty of the Earth: Women, Sacramentality, and Justice*, among others.

Contributors

Todd A. Salzman is the Amelia and Emil Graff Professor of Catholic Theology at Creighton University. He is the author of many books, many coauthored by Michael Lawler, including *The Sexual Person* and *Pope Francis, Marriage, and Same-Sex Civil Unions*.

Cristina L. H. Traina is Avery Cardinal Dulles, SJ, Professor of Catholic Theology at Fordham University. She is the author of *Finitude, Feminism, and Flourishing: On Being Mortal Like Everyone Else* and *Feminist Ethics and Natural Law*, among others.